This book belongs to:

____

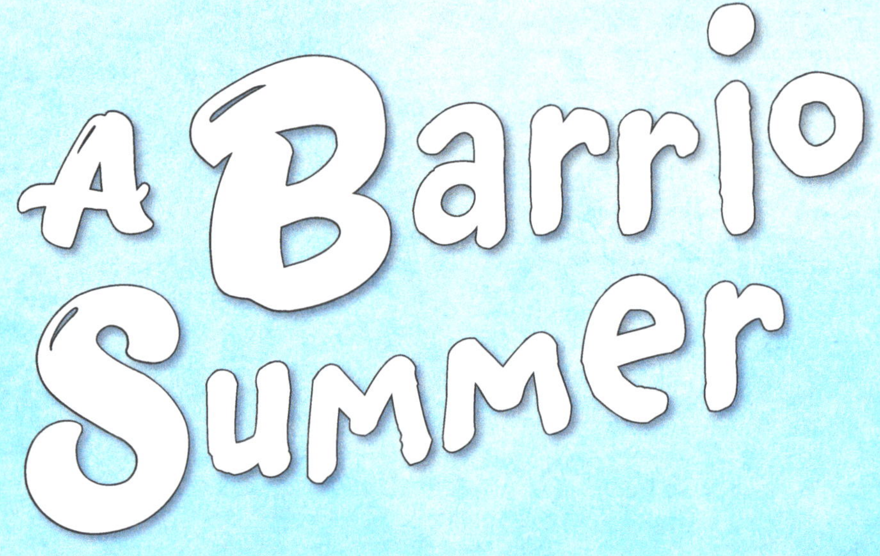

For our children and the children of the barrio, may your stories always be affirmed.

— Edna & Lisa

A Barrio Summer

Written by Edna Iglesias

First Edition: August, 2024

ISBN: 979-8-218-48472-9

Published by Edna Iglesias,
San Antonio, Texas

Cover design by Lisa G De Leon
Book design by Dusty Rockets

Printed in the United States of America

The best place during summer break was in the barrio on Bay Street.

It didn't require travel of any kind. No plane tickets, reservations, or packing needed.

Every summer, Bay Street, which was sandwiched between two rows of humble homes on each side, transformed into a creative arena and sports multiplex for all the children who lived there.

FINISH

At one end of the street there was a tall aluminum fence, which the kids used as the finish line for all running and bike races. It was also the home base of many games of tag.

The kids of Bay Street spent most mornings and early afternoons in their backyards or inside, shielding themselves from the Texas heat.

The backyard metal swing-sets hosted daily Olympic games like swing jumps and bar flips.

During peak heat times, plastic pools provided hours of refreshing fun under the canopy of a large Mesquite tree.

Here, the backyard Olympics continued with games like water somersault contests, underwater penny searches, and breath-holding competitions.

The backyard games were often followed by an indoor rest time and snack. Children lay on the cold vinyl floor to cool their bodies as they watched cartoons and TV show reruns.

There was never a shortage of cold, fresh fruit topped with lime juice and chili powder to enjoy.

This was the quietest time on Bay Street.

Summer was full of sunny days that were dry and humid, but sometimes those days were blessed with afternoon Texas thunderstorms that cooled the air with large cold drops of rain.

The window to enjoy the rain was a short one. The kids had to be ready to catch the rain before the thunder rolled in or before the sun peeked out again.

Most spun on the lawn with arms stretched out like helicopter blades, their smiling faces pointing toward the sky under the crisp rainfall.

When no afternoon showers were in sight, a different sort of treat rolled onto Bay Street, playing a concert of xylophone melodies.

The concert on wheels lured kids out of their homes in search of raspas, paletas, nieves and oodles of sweet and sour candies.

Kids searched for loose change forgotten by parents under sofa cushions or entryway tables to pay for the treats.

Ice Cream

After dinner was the busiest time on Bay Street. The older kids played games of kickball or basketball and rode their bikes past the stop sign at the end of the street.

The younger children jumped from one lawn game to another, playing Chinese jump rope, jacks, hide-and-seek, hopscotch, and imaginary play at the outdoor kitchen.

The menu of the barrio summer kitchen included mud cakes adorned with honeysuckle flower petals and laurel leaf tacos with a mud filling and grass clippings.

All this counted down to the evening game of tag.

The game started when the older kids rode back onto Bay Street, wheeling onto the green lawns. They jumped off their bikes and made a mad dash to the manguera.

This "drinking fountain" required skills. Drinkers had to let the water run from the hose for a few seconds to avoid burning their mouths with the sun-heated water. But after a brief wait came a thirst-quenching stream of cool water.

The drink was followed by a quick splash to the face and then a call of ***"Let's go!"***

With the bikes lying on the lawns, all the kids, regardless of age, came together in the middle of the street to start a game of freeze tag.

It was a well-orchestrated game with unwritten rules. Everyone knew the rules and followed them, to allow the game to continue past sunset.

After the sun went down, the streetlamps came alive to illuminate Bay Street.

Soon the porch lights to the homes followed. One by one, each light served as a beacon, calling each kid home for the night.

As each barrio summer day came to an end, one thing was certain:

they would do it all again tomorrow.

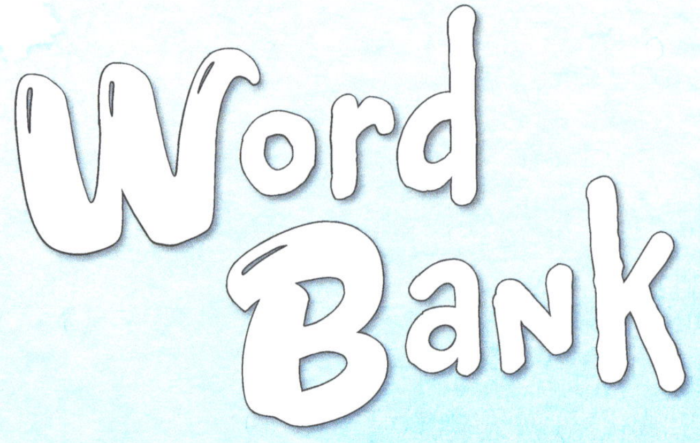

Barrio:........................Neighborhood

Manguera:..................Garden Hose

Nieves:........................Ice Cream

Paletas:.......................Popsicles

Raspas:.......................Snow Cones

A Barrio Summer

www.ingramcontent.com/pod-product-compliance
Lightning Source LLC
LaVergne TN
LVHW071130160826
845679LV00005B/1234
* 9 7 9 8 2 1 8 4 8 4 7 2 9 *